Matthe

MY
Destiny

TRILOGY
A WHOLLY OWNED SUBSIDIARY OF **TBN**
PROFESSIONAL PUBLISHING MEETS POWERFUL PROMOTION

10 9 8 7 6 5 4 3 2 1
Library of Congress Cataloging-in-Publication Data is available.
ISBN 979-8-89333-679-5
ISBN 979-8-89333-680-1 (ebook)

Acknowledgments

A special thanks to my father Howard Aarons and my mother Violet Aarons, who have been a great source of love and direction, provision, and protection. To my mom, dad, and brother: you have molded my life into what it is today. I have much gratitude for your selfless and efficacious devotion to me and the Aarons family.

Much thanks to Mark Mingle and the TBN/Trilogy family for this opportunity.

Thanks to my marching band director Evan Rogovin, who imparted musical knowledge to me in my high school years.

To songwriter Richard Smallwood, who influenced my composing and songwriting as a gospel music artist.

To my primary school teacher Miss Patricia Gardner, who taught me the importance of education in my formative years in Jamaica.

To the classical music composers who have influenced my writing: Johann Sebastian Bach and Amadeus Mozart.

Thanks to Pentecostal Tabernacle International, and to the late S. Robert Stewart.

Foreword

We are not certain if it was before or after he was born that the meaning of his name resonated so much with us. Matthew is certainly a "gift from God." God has gifted him with a passion for music, writing songs, and a love for the Word of God. He has met many challenges in his young life, but the Lord is taking him through. God has inspired him to chronicle the highs and lows of the path to his eternal destiny.

As his parents, we are thankful for this gift. We pray that God's divine purpose be fulfilled in his life. We know that this book will help people everywhere, especially young people, to understand that the path to our divine destiny may be filled with perils, turmoil, challenges, and valley experiences. We should take courage in the fact that "if God brings us to it, He will bring us through it."

Howard and Violet Aarons

Table of Contents

My Beginnings

On February 19, 1988, a bubbly baby boy was born in St. Ann's Bay Hospital in Jamaica to Violet and Howard Aarons. I grew up in Windsor Heights, St. Ann, and I later moved to Great Pond Ocho Rios, Jamaica. I was dedicated at Calvary Tabernacle United Pentecostal Church, where bishop David Gallimore was the pastor. Church was a major part of my life. Dad and Mom made sure we attended church every Sunday morning, and not attending was not an option. I can remember the choir singing one of their selections, "Ride On, King Jesus," and another selection on a Sunday night service was "Move, Mountain." The Holy Spirit definitely visited our service when those songs were sung. It was on a Sunday night service where I was filled with the precious Holy Spirit at the age of six, and I was later baptized in the name of Jesus Christ.

I've always had a love for music. At a young age, I can remember taking wooden hangers and using them as drumsticks and using my foot as the pedal, pretending I was giving a grand concert where I was the featured artist. I sang in the Sunday school choir and often played the drums for the choir as well. My mom noticed my passion for music and sent me to take piano lessons at Sam Sharpe Music School in Ocho Rios, Jamaica. There I learned the basics of piano; reading music was not one of my fond memories, because I learned to pick up music by ear. Another passion of mine was track and field, where I was the fastest athlete and a sprinter when we had field day at my primary school, St Ann's Bay Primary. I attended Miracle Tabernacle basic school. I can remember taking the bus to school, and I would walk the rest of the journey to school. God reminded me that He would be with me to protect me through the journey of life. The Lord also reminded me that if I walk with Him, He will be with me through the journey of life.

Growing up, I was often asthmatic and had to be rushed to the hospital on occasion because of its severity. I remember having the nebulizer and the asthma pump that I was prescribed by my doctor. It was my mom, Violet, who was there with me through these illnesses, I remember, mostly at night, weathering the storm and sickness. I remember one night I was sick, severely, and it was me and my dad, and I can remember telling my dad, "Don't cry, Daddy, don't cry; pray, Daddy, pray." At that young age I recognized the power of prayer and God's power to heal. And I can say through it all, I can trust in Jesus; through it all, I can trust in God. Nevertheless, later on I was healed by God from asthma. I am greatly thankful for

God's healing hand upon my life. I remember also having a hernia and was advised by my doctor for it to be surgically removed. I remember quite vividly that my father anointed me and prayed for me for the hernia to be removed, and not many days later the Lord miraculously touched my body, and I was healed.

My father broke the news to us that we had been filed to reside in the United States by our Aunt Chevy. My brother Aldane and my mother and I all agreed to migrate to the United States to live. It was off to New Jersey, where we journeyed to a new environment. Sister Taylor and Brother Taylor were kind to us, and we found our new home in Clifton, New Jersey. We moved in 2002 and found a new church home in True Witness Apostolic Church in Paterson, New Jersey. In New Jersey I found my new passion for the piano. Out of nowhere I felt the urge to ask my dad to purchase a piano. Hearing this, my dad asked me if I was sure about purchasing a piano; however, I reassured him and told him I was sure. We went to Sam Ash and purchased my first piano, a PSR Yamaha 61-key keyboard. This was at the cusp of my musical journey, and I started learning to play the piano by ear and simply by watching tutorials online; by the help of God, I was self-taught to play the piano. All I knew was what a C major chord was, which was taught to me by my piano teacher. In New Jersey, I attended Christopher Columbus Middle School. I remember I would walk in the freezing cold to attend school. Shortly after I graduated from middle school, since my parents were not accustomed to the cold, we took a very long journey by bus to sunny South Florida. As a family we were still getting acclimatized to a new environment; however, Florida was a lot like Jamaica, so we adjusted to being in Florida. In Florida I attended Santaluces High School, where I had memorable moments. I joined the marching band, where I had some of the best moments of my life. In marching band I was in the pit, where I played the drum set, and later on I joined the drumline, playing bass drums. Under the leadership and direction of Evan Rogovin, we spent hours rehearsing after school to make sure our marching band was the best as we strived for a spirit of excellence. I enjoyed playing various selections with my bandmates at various football games for our high school. We came in first place in the 4A band competition at state.

Right before my brother Aldane enlisted to go into the navy I experienced what is called a spiritual attack, where the enemy wanted to inflict me with an anxiety disorder. On many occasions I had a racing heart, sweaty palms, and discomfort and oppression. Fear wanted to take charge of my life, and oftentimes I would be in mental anguish. Nevertheless, I was reminded of the scripture that says that God has not given us a spirit of fear, but of power, love, and a sound mind (2 Timothy 1:7). As a result of anxiety, I was diagnosed with chronic acid reflux disease. I lost a lot of weight because of acid reflux and had to be placed on medication, which was Nexium. However, the medication did not help; I still had difficulty swallowing solid foods and at one point had to be placed on a liquid diet. I felt like the woman with the issue of blood who had had this disease for a number of years but had spent all the money she had on the doctor; instead of getting better, the disease was chronic and grew worse. I later did an endoscopy to dilate my esophagus because of the acid erosions. We had thought that the surgery would have helped, but the acid reflux still persisted.

After I graduated high school I later attended Palm Beach State College, where I studied computer science. Around this transition of my life, my father became pastor of Pentecostal Tabernacle of West Palm Beach. Our church was in a school where we gathered every Sunday to have service. I became the music director for my dad's church, and we had rehearsals every Saturday. As a result of our church being in a school, I remember packing out the musical instruments, which includes speaker monitors, from storage and setting up and connecting cables to the sound system that we had. Sometimes I packed out this heavy equipment by myself.

Later, with the help of our mother church, we finally purchased a church of our own. It was a real estate office, so it was necessary that we do reconstruction. So, the workers in the church worked tirelessly to reconstruct the beautiful church that we now have. We also had to carry the musical equipment from the school where we had church to our new church home. So, the church was finally coming together with the sound room to the back; the carpet was placed in the sanctuary and the rostrum was installed; and our Hammond organ was in place and drums, keyboards, and praise team mic stands were installed. The chairs in the pews were in place, and the church had a fragrance that I will never forget. Now it was time for our church to be dedicated and start the beginning of a new season in ministry. Our bishop Robert Stewart and his brother Sammy Stewart were there for the dedication, and an indelible mark they had given to us and granted to my father to lead a flock in this new season. The Lord gave me a song to write entitled "Fill This Temple." Upon my bed I opened my Bible, and the book and chapter that I stumbled upon was 2 Chronicles 5:14, where at the dedication of the temple in the Old Testament, the priest could not stand to minister because of the presence of God. That song was divinely inspired for the season that our church was in, and that's the song that the Lord gave me and the song that the choir ministered at our dedication service.

Calling from God

In 2012 I had an encounter with God that changed my life: as I was sleeping, I heard the voice of Christ saying, "Speak what I have given you to speak." I heard those words three times. It was so surreal, because here I was in this modern generation—I never expected an audible voice of Christ calling me to preach. Those words literally woke me up from my sleep, and I shouted, "The blood of Jesus!" I just started pleading the blood of Jesus because that call was loud and thunderous and quite unexpected. That call was unexpected because I had delivered a sermon on a Sunday night, and I felt I didn't do that sermon justice, and I felt embarrassed because I thought the people didn't receive my preaching and I was not applauded for my efforts. The call led me on a twenty-one day fast where I had communion with Christ, and at that time I worked as a tutor at Palm Beach State College. I would fast from 6 a.m. to 6 p.m. and I prayed three times a day. I fasted not only because I heard the voice of the Lord, but because I needed to be healed from acid reflux disease and I was desperate for a healing. During the fast my spiritual eyes opened up, and I could see angels in my room just like the scripture says in Isaiah chapter 6: with two wings they covered their eyes, with two wings they covered their feet, and with two wings they did fly. My features started to change during this fast; it was as if my face was glowing—there was a light that emanated from within and shone through my face. I could feel the fire of God's presence on my life during these days of consecration. I could see angels by the praise team mics. During this period, I could feel the Holy Spirit hovering on me and around me. It was almost as if God was pouring out His people within my vessel, my temple, and anointing me with oil. That's what the anointing really means—it means to rub or to smear with oil.

Just as the scripture says, the Jews have zeal but not according to knowledge. I never realized that the enemy would come to attack my health and my body during these days of fasting. Just as Jesus went into the wilderness to fast and be tempted by the evil one, that's how I felt. I was on my job and it was as if I was hallucinating—hearing voices, but it was not God's voice. Little did I know that during this fast my blood sugar fell low, and I had to be rushed to the hospital as a result. Even though I was getting results from this fast, I was also ignorant of the enemy's devices. I want to encourage readers that we have to know that we are not spirit, we are mortal flesh; and we are not immortal, we are also physical; we should use wisdom and not be heavenly minded with no earthly good. When I came from the hospital during hypoglycemia, low blood sugar, I went to sleep in the midst of what was experiencing, and I could feel a warm and slightly hot hand on my back. Beloved, in the midst of this sickness, the hand of God was upon me and ministering unto me in the midst of my trial.

Nevertheless, the power of God was upon me during preaching, and no longer would I have to struggle to find a message or to deliver a message, but the Holy Spirit would come upon me and inspire me during my sermons and give me the words to preach. During 2012 I preached at my first youth conference that my church was hosting, and the theme of the conference was "The Hour of Refining." This title was so impactful because that was exactly what I was going through—a time of purification and the trying of my faith. Gold has to go through the fire in order to come out pure. The power of God was in that conference, and lives were touched. The sermons were entitled "The Power of the Holy Ghost," "Don't Give Up On the Lord," "You Shall Live and Not Die," "Back to Eden," "Let God Take Control," "So You Want to Be Blessed," "Three Stages of Prayer," "Repent Now," and "Push for Your Anointing." All these sermons I preached by the help of the Holy Spirit without a script—they were all unscripted without any notes, because the Holy Spirit told me, like the Lord said to Ezekiel in Ezekiel 3:27 (NIV), "I will open your mouth," and not to be afraid of men's faces, but to preach whether the people want to hear or whether they will not hear.

The Crucible

On March 31, 2013, I experienced severe spiritual warfare. It was easter Sunday, where I had preached a sermon about the birth, death, burial, and resurrection of the Christ, where I was attacked by the enemy—where I felt an "Ichabod," where I felt the spirit and presence of God had departed from me. This was the most painful, most excruciating experience I have ever had. This experience caused me to lose my ability to drive my car and to do simple tasks that the average human being is able to do. I felt like the psalmist David in that season, where he said, "Cast me not away from thy presence; and take not thy holy spirit from me" (Psalm 51:11 KJV). This experience caused me to sever my relationship with my parents and move to the city of Atlanta, Georgia. I got my ears pierced and had little or no interest in preaching or living for God. This experience caused me to go into the environment of partying and drinking. I had little or no desire for God, because I felt a void and an emptiness within that could only be satisfied by the pleasures of world and what it had to offer. I felt bitter and angry at God because I was obeying the call of God on my life—preaching, evangelizing, and witnessing, going door to door, praying that souls would heed the call of God and be saved. I felt like Job, where I lost everything and was being taunted by the enemy, saying that if God loved me, He would not have allowed me to go through my trial. At one instance I was living in poverty, living in a motel in Atlanta, and I felt like the prodigal son who had wasted all his inheritance on partying and riotous living. At one point I was sleeping in my car with all my belongings, because I had no place to live and I did not have any money to pay to stay at a motel. At this season in my life I was gigging at different churches in Atlanta to earn an income, but couldn't commit to the job because I was plagued with various illnesses including paranoia, hallucinations, anxiety, and depression. In this season I was also plagued by insomnia and had difficulty sleeping. Beloved, I was experiencing a maze and a minefield of conundrums that caused me not to be living in the blessing of Abraham, like God promised to Israel.

Like the prodigal, I came to my senses and returned to my father's house. Even though I had returned, I still felt as though I was not called to preach or even to play an instrument. I would sit at the back in the sound room, having no desire to hear the droppings and preaching of God's Word. I was in a backslidden state, and I felt distant from God. I can remember at a conference that my church had, I was given an opportunity to give a sermonette by a mighty woman of God, and beloved, in that moment I felt the power of God that I had felt back when the hand of God was upon my back in 2012 and 2013. Mind you, I did not plan to give a sermonette, and I was not notified that I should speak, but the Holy Spirit in that moment inspired me to tell the people about Christ in the midst of the golden candlesticks in the book of Revelation, where the candlesticks represent the Church and Christ being in the Church. I stated that we are having church but God is outside, knocking, trying to come in. And that is true in our churches today—that we are having church but God's presence is not among us.

Just like the saying goes: the higher you go, the more the attack comes. I often experienced auditory hallucinations. I could see, as it were, ghosts or spirits trying to come against my peace. As a result of these hallucinations I had to be back at the hospital. There, I spent weeks trying to get better and overcome this trial. Through these trials and days in the hospital, I understood the importance of God's Word and His power to keep and to preserve us when we are at our lowest point. "For I reckon that the sufferings of this present time are not worthy to be compared with the glory which shall be revealed in us" (Romans 8:18 KJV).

My biggest influences on my ministry are Noel Jones, Oral Roberts, and Kathryn Kuhlman. I can remember falling asleep listening to Noel Jones's sermons, and I was intrigued by the healing ministry of Oral Roberts, and during my trials I would listen and imbibe his teaching and his healing crusades. Kathryn Kuhlman was also a big influence in my life as well, and how God used her as a point of contact to minister healing to the masses.

An uncle of mine told me that Aarons, my last name, is of Jewish decent, and that my family on my dad's side came from Israel and later migrated to Jamaica. Jamaica has a rich Jewish heritage, and there is a synagogue in Kingston. Jamaicans with the last name Cohen, Abrahams, Isaacs, Jacobs, Levi, and Levy are most likely of Jewish ancestry. Jews fled from Spain because of the Spanish Inquisition and fled to Jamaica in order to flee persecution. I am very proud of my Jewish heritage and embrace the promises and covenants that God made to Israel. I'm reminded of the scripture that says, "And he shall purify the sons of Levi" (Malachi 3:3 KJV).

Being a gospel artist, pianist, and composer was not always easy; being a gospel artist often costs a lot of money to promote and market. I have written and recorded songs such as "My Peace," "Glorious," and "Fear Not." These songs speak to me every time I listen back to them, because they comfort in times where there is turmoil, and especially remind me not to fear despite what situation or circumstances I may face. I have also composed and written a piano concerto symphony for an orchestra that I desire to have in concert someday. Some of my gospel musical influences are Richard Smallwood, James Hall, and Kurt Carr, who have inspired how I write and compose my songs. They have that classical sound which I love and admire. I'm inspired by classical composers such as Johan Sebastian Bach, Mozart, Rachmaninov, Verdi, and Chopin. Some of my favorite contemporary classical pianists are Khatia Buniatishvili, Yuja Wang, Helene Grimaud, and Martha Algerich. Musicians are often considered weird or odd because we operate at a different frequency than other individuals, because we thrive off of inspiration and the enemy often attacks our inspiration.

The death of my grandmother Winnifred Parke was one of the most horrendous experiences I've had in this life. Because "Miss Cookie," as she was affectionately known, was always a tower of strength to our family. I can remember her love for plants and flowers, and how she would prune and water those flowers in her garden. After school we would go to her house when we had our youth conference later on in the evening, and she would cook for us and make sure we taken care of. Nevertheless, I am reminded of the scripture, "Behold, I show you a mystery: we shall not all sleep, but we shall all be changed, in a moment, in the twinkling of an eye" (1 Corinthians 15:51-52 KJV). This is the consolation that I have—that I shall see her again in the sweet by and by. In a place where there is no sorrow, where we shall rest from all our labor, and we shall see King Jesus in heaven and reign with Him forever. What a hope and a blessed consolation we have as believers, that we shall see our loved ones again.

I've always had an affinity for and a longing to love and

to be loved; however, my experiences with romance seem to be far-fetched. The scripture says in Genesis 2:24 to leave mother and father and cleave to one's wife. However, my experiences seem to be roses with thorns amidst my life, wanting to grasp ahold of love; but I seem to be wounded by relationships that I thought were concrete and meaningful. It appears to me that people are fickle and conditional; as a result, that's why there are so many divorced individuals. So, I desire to give myself to God, who will never leave me nor forsake me; and Christ's love was to die for, and His love is unconditional. Ever since I was a child, and into adulthood, I've always had few friends and often seem to find myself alone and in isolation. Nevertheless, in the midst of the isolation were my parents, Howard and Violet, who have loved me endlessly and shown me that true love exists and was promulgated to me through my day-to-day situations. Beloved readers, I am a testament to God's faithfulness and His power to keep you even at your lowest point. Though you may seem to want to give up and throw in the towel, let these words be a reminder to you that God has you in His hands, and though the vessels seem marred in the hands of the Potter, He will never throw away the clay but will mold and fashion you into a finished product which is beautiful.

Theology

———

I've always had a passion for the doctrinal construct of theology, which is the study of God. From Genesis to Revelation, God has always been a part of humanity. And oftentimes we are led to question if God is real and tangible, because everything we see tells us not to believe. But we must understand that God is outside of our rationale and intellect. We cannot put God under a microscope to figure Him out; we have to utilize faith to have a relationship with God. By faith we believe that the world was framed by the word of God; faith is the bridge that takes us to God. You may be going through a trial that causes you to question if God is; my friends, God knows your end from your beginning, and before you were formed in your mother's womb God knew you, and God knew that trial that you're going through. We must understand that God is a spirit and He is eternal; before there was time, God existed. He is the self-existing, ever-present God. God is omnipresent, meaning that He is everywhere at the same time. God is omniscient, which means He knows everything. God is omnipotent, which means He has all power. *Katabole,* in the Greek, means throwing down or laying down. So, God *katabole*'d the earth and created everything therein, and created man in His own image. So let's set the record straight, that in the beginning God created the heavens and the earth. The earth was not formed by chance or happenstance, or by a big bang theory, but God created all things.

We as finite beings question God as to why there is death, why there is suffering, why there is pain. And if God loves me, why have all of these problems overtaken me? The answer to those questions is that God is sovereign. God allows us to go through situations and trials and tribulations. God allowed Job to go through his test, where the enemy took away his children and his source of income and touched his body with sores. Even though Job went through his trial, he never cursed God, even though his wife was persuading him to charge God foolishly. We have to be careful not to listen to people around us when we go through our trials, because they will try to cause us to curse God and blame God for what we are going through. Job's friends said it was his sin that caused him to go through his trial, but Job had not sinned against God. Sometimes God tests good people; it was the goodness and uprightness of Job that moved the wicked one against Job. We must learn to praise God in the midst of what we are going through. Job said, "The Lord gave, and the Lord hath taken away;

blessed be the name of the Lord" (Job 1:21 KJV).

There are various names of God; one is Jehovah Jireh, which means "God who provides." So, if there is any lack in your life, just remember that God who provides is able to give you a supernatural blessing. When the children of Israel were in the wilderness, wandering without food or water, God rained down manna from heaven and the children of Israel were sustained. Jehovah Rapha means "the God who heals," so if you have an ailment or a disease, remember that God is able to heal you. Jehovah Shalom means "God of peace," so if you are depressed or oppressed, just know that God is able to give you peace that passes all human understanding. Jehovah Nissi means "God our banner," so if you need protection and feel surrounded by circumstances, and the enemy of our souls seems to surround you, just remember that God is able to protect you from the enemy. One of my favorite names for God is Jehovah Sabaoth, which means "the God of angel armies." Just know that God has angels dispatched around the believer and nothing can penetrate that protection. The angel of the Lord encamps around them that fear Him. There is a host of angelic beings that are around the believer.

Christology

Christology is the study of Jesus Christ, and shows Christ's purpose here on earth. Sin gave Jesus purpose here on earth, and the reason for Him coming to earth was to save us from the condemnation and judgment of sin. "For God so loved the world that He gave His only begotten Son, that whoever believes in Him should not perish but have everlasting life." It was love that God was manifested in the flesh to save us from ourselves. Love is the golden text of the Bible, and all things hang on this verse in John 3:16 (NKJV). I have always struggled with my flesh and its desires and often felt guilty after sinning, and the psychology of sin often caused me to feel depressed and unworthy of God's mercies. However, I'm reminded of the scripture that says, "For God hath not appointed us to wrath, but to obtain salvation by our Lord Jesus Christ" (1 Thessalonians 5:9 KJV). God did not save us to send us to a place where we are separated from God for all eternity, but to be in bliss with God eternally. Grace is God's unmerited favor, God's undeserved favor, that even though we sin, God's blood makes atonement for us. No longer do we have to offer up a blood sacrifice of lambs and bulls, but the blood of Jesus Christ when He we was whipped; and they put a crown of thorns on His head, and they pierced Christ in the side and blood and water came out. When He was on the cross, he cried, "My God, my God, why hast Thou forsaken me?" (Matthew 27:46 KJV). Beloved, our sins and transgressions will He remember no more because of the salvific work on the cross. Jesus died for our sins, past, present, and future, and no man can pluck us out of His hand. If we say that we have no sin, we lie, and the truth of God is not in us, "For all have sinned and fall short of the glory of God" (Romans 3:23 NKJV). "There is therefore now no condemnation to them which are in Christ Jesus" (Romans 8:1 KJV). Hence we should not feel condemned if we sin; all we have to do is repent, if we have fallen, to get back in the race and keep running.

I have always been fascinated and intrigued by the doctrine of eschatology. Eschatology is the doctrine of the end times and last things. The last days will be an exciting time for the church but will be hard times for unbelievers. In the book of Joel, God promised to pour out His Spirit upon all flesh; sons and daughters shall prophesy, and old men shall dream dreams, and young men shall see visions (Joel 2:28). Some scholars and theologians believe that the church will be raptured before the great tribulation, and some theologians believe that the church will go through the tribulation. Beloved, God has not appointed us unto wrath, but to receive salvation through our Lord Jesus Christ. The word *rapture* is not in the Bible, but the apostle Paul uses the words "caught up" in 1Thessalonians 4:17. *Rapture* simply means the snatching away of the church who are ready and a state of preparedness for Christ's return. The Bible gave us certain precursors and a foreshadowing of the end times. A foreshadowing of the end times is that men will be lovers of themselves, and we have seen a sense of selfishness in men in this present day. The apostle Paul warns us of perilous times ahead, wars and rumors of wars. Matthew 24 warns us of these perilous and dreadful times ahead. In the end times, the Bible warns us of wars and rumors of wars and earthquakes in diverse places, and we have seen these prophecies being fulfilled. As believers, we don't have to be fearful of these perilous days but to be prepared for the unknown day that God will return to reign as King of kings and Lord of lords. We are just pilgrims and sojourners, and we have a home in heaven with God.

Another prophecy of the end times is a great falling away, a falling away from being steadfast and spiraling down into a backslidden state. We have seen where a lot of the Millennials and Gen Z young people have left the church, and they have no desire to live for God. However, there will be a remnant of young people on whom the Lord is going to pour out His Spirit in the end times. In the book of Revelation, it states that the stars from heaven shall fall and the moon shall turn into blood (Revelation 6:12-

13). We often sing the song "Awake, Zion, awake, awake and trim your lamps," and we as the church have to be sober and vigilant, knowing that at any moment the Lord Jesus will return to the earth. Revelation talks about seven years of tribulation, three and a half years of peace, and three and a half years of peril, where that wicked one, the lawless dictator, will be revealed. During the tribulation 144 thousand Jews will be sealed during the tribulation. Revelation also talks about the ten thousand times ten thousand that John saw in heaven, which means that there will be a remnant that will be saved and will be raptured that will be arrayed in white garments, singing, "Worthy is the Lamb... slain from the foundation of the world" (Revelation 5:12, 13:8 KJV). Scripture states that we need to pray for the nation of Israel, because they will seek refuge from the nations of the world in the end times and they will face severe persecution from the ungodly nations.

Death—I've come to understand that it's a part of life, and I've always wanted to look at what the scripture says about the afterlife. Jesus said that He is the resurrection and life; he that believeth in Him, though he were dead, yet shall he live, and he that believeth in Him will never die. As Christians, we have a hope of living again after this physical life is over, and maybe you might have lost a loved one and are dealing with grief. For us as believers we rejoice, as the scripture says in Revelation, that "blessed are the dead which die in the Lord from henceforth... they may rest from their labors; and their works do follow them"

(Revelation 14:13 KJV). So, there is a blessing in death, and we need not sorrow when we lose a loved one who was saved and knew God. Jesus proved Himself as the resurrection and the life when he raised Lazarus from the dead, so when the trumpet sounds, the dead in Christ shall rise to meet the Lord in the air. The apostle Paul declares, "Behold, I show you a mystery: we shall not all sleep, but we shall be changed in a moment, in the twinkling of an eye" (1 Corinthians 15:51-52 paraphrased). This brings us to the destination one goes to when one dies. There is a place of peace and happiness for those who die in Christ, and there is a place of torment for those who have rejected God in their lifetime. The Bible records the story of the rich man and Lazarus, which shows the two destinations that people go to based on how they lived in this life. Lazarus died and was carried into Abraham's bosom; the rich man died and was buried. Lazarus's life on earth wasn't pleasant, and he was in poverty; however, Lazarus received eternal life in heaven even though he was poor. Salvation is not based on how much money we possess or the material things that we gain in this life, but it is by being poor in spirit and living our lives in humility that we may be accepted by God in heaven.

Angels that Help Us

In my study of angelology, I have been fascinated by angels and their function. Angels are God's emissaries, God's representatives that function on God's behalf. Angels are recorded in Genesis, when God said, "Let us make man in our image" (Genesis 1:26 KJV). Angels were also seen guarding the Garden of Eden after Adam and Eve sinned and were put out. An angel appeared unto Sarai about the promised seed after being barren for many years. Angels appeared unto to Abraham to warn of an impending judgment on Sodom and Gomora. Jacob saw angels ascending and descending on a ladder, and he called that place Bethel. Jacob also wrestled with an angel, and his walk changed, and his hip was put out of joint, and his name was changed to Israel. Beloved, any man that comes in contact with God will never be the same. In the book of Exodus, an angel went ahead of the children of Israel to lead them out of Egypt from the bondmen of Pharoah. An angel came to Samson's mother to give her a message that Samson shall be a Nazarite. Samson was given the instruction that he should not cut his hair and he should not drink any strong drink, because of his anointing. An angel was sent to Daniel when he went on a twenty-one day fast; this angel was exquisite, and his face was like lightning, and his voice was like a host of people. This angel was sent to Daniel to strengthen him and to give him a message that the moment Daniel set himself to pray, his prayers were heard by God. Through your situation, God will send an angel to strengthen you in the midst of your weakness. In Isaiah chapter six, verse 3 (KJV), the prophet Isaiah saw seraphim which had six wings, and they cried, "Holy, holy, holy is the Lord of hosts: the whole earth is full of his glory." Ezekiel saw angelic beings with a man's face, with a lion's face, and with an eagle's face. The lion's face represents war and dominion; the eagle's face represents sight and foresight and vision. The man's face represents humanity and authority. The scripture declares that He will give His angels charge over thee, to keep thee in all thy ways—so when you are on the job, when you are at home, when you are in the supermarket, angels are commissioned by God to protect you. The reason why you did not die in that car accident is because angels were at work. The reason why you didn't fall off the bed during sleep at night is because angels are watching over you and protecting you while you sleep. As I drove from a youth lock-in that they had at our mother church in Miami Gardens, I fell asleep at the steering wheel of my car, and I don't know how I got home—but when I woke up, I found myself in my neighborhood. Jehovah Sabaoth was at work to drive me safely home. God will always be our Jehovah Nissi, our banner and protection. Elisha asked God to open the eyes of the young man that he may see a host of angels surrounding them (2 Kings 6:17). Sometimes God has to touch our natural eyes to see the invisible spirit realm of angels. For angels are ministering spirits to the heirs of salvation.

In order for an olive tree to be produced, the olive has to be crushed. In order for grapevines to produce grapes, the grape has to be crushed. You may feel like you are being crushed and pressed beyond measure; just know that in God's eyes, the crushing is a part of the process. Maybe you lost a loved one, or maybe you are experiencing a disease in your body; just know that the crushing is a part of being anointed. The anointing oil flows when there is pain and turmoil. The Garden of Gethsemane is significant because it is where Christ spent His last hours before His death and crucifixion. Jesus prayed till His sweat became drops of blood, and Jesus cried, "Let this cup pass from me" (Matthew 26:39 KJV). Knowing that His hour of death had come, knowing that He would be betrayed with a kiss by Judas Iscariot, Christ felt crushed beyond measure— knowing the embarrassment, knowing that He would be whipped and spat upon. Beloved, there are some of you that the Lord wants to place an anointing upon your life; nevertheless, the crushing is a part of the process. I have been through so much pain in my life that I had to ask the Lord why, but I had to understand: "much pain; much power."

Theophany

I've always wondered what God looks like, what He sounds like, what His personality is like. God's desire is to reveal Himself to his servants, and oftentimes we don't see or hear Him because we have not taken the time to listen to His voice. In Genesis, God would commune with Adam in the cool of the day, and I believe that Adam saw His face and heard the distinction of God's voice. In the book of Exodus, God revealed Himself to Moses at the back side of the mountain. God tends to reveal Himself to those who are in isolation, who are by themselves. Sometimes we need to shut out the noise of people's opinions and tune in to what God has to say. Moses was the only prophet that saw God face to face; every other prophet God spoke to mouth to mouth. Moses saw God's face at the burning bush and was called up on the mountain, where the children of Israel heard and saw thunder and lightning, which caused them to be afraid. Beloved, if we are to see the face of God, most times it requires a sacrifice, and God's presence will cause us to be afraid. God's presence is powerful and awesome, to the point where Moses had to cover his face with a veil because Moses' face shone, and the people who saw him were afraid. Oh, that we would have a desire to be in the presence of God and a heart to pursue Him, for He is not far from any one of us; "for in him we live, and move, and have our being" (Acts 17:28 KJV).

Ezekiel the prophet saw a wheel in the middle of a wheel and saw the train of God's glory fill the temple. In this instance, Ezekiel was called to be a prophet to the nation of Israel. Ezekiel also saw a vision of God, as it were, an epiphany of the Almighty, and he saw an appearance of fire from his loins, even downward fire, and an appearance of brightness and a color of amber. We must understand that God is a consuming fire, and we all need the fire of God to purify us and change us into His image. We all should pray that God would remove the veil from our eyes and gives us a glimpse into His presence. Ezekiel also saw the throne of God and a man clothed with linen, and smoke filled the temple, and there were cherubim; the sound of their wings was as the voice of the Almighty when He speaks.

Kingdom Economics

God, in the garden, provided sustenance for Adam and Eve. Sin is the cause of us working and laboring on the job because of Adam and Eve's transgressions. God's desire and intention was for mankind not to work but to live in paradise. When man sinned, God said, "By the sweat of your brow you shall eat bread" (Genesis 3:19 LEB). The Our Father prayer states, "Give us this day our daily bread" (Matthew 6:11 NKJV), which means that God is the provider of food for the nourishment of our bodies, because we cannot survive without food. We were not created like machines that do not need to eat. God provided for the children of Israel in the wilderness. God provided manna, which was angels' food which came down supernaturally from heaven. God also fed them quails, which were birds sent by God so the children of Israel could eat. God tests us as times to see if we will trust Him in our wilderness experience. We must have faith to believe that God has the capacity to provide a supernatural blessing for His people.

The children of Israel were murmuring and complaining that it was better for them to be in Egypt because they had no food in the wilderness. It is interesting to note that the children of Israel saw the mighty hand of God when He opened the Red Sea, but still they forgot how God brought them out of their bondage. We need to remember the things that God has done for us in the past and reflect on His goodness. I have been in various situations where I needed God to provide monetarily to pay the bills; it is in scripture that money answers to all things. However, I reflect on God's Word that the cattle on a thousand hills are His, and "the earth is the Lord's and the fullness thereof" (1 Corinthians 10:26 KJV). The resources of God's economy will never go bankrupt; God's resources are endless.

Remember that we are the seed of Abraham, and he has made a covenant with God's heir. "Blessing will I bless you, and multiplying will I multiply your descendants" (Genesis 22:17 KJV). God says we are the head and not the tail, above and not beneath, the lender and not the borrower. God's words are sure, and we can stand on His promises. God said our store baskets will be full, and they will overflow in abundance. When there was famine in Israel in the time of the prophet Elijah, God sent a raven to sustain him. God also sustained him through a brook of water. It's important that we understand location is important, because there is a location where God has a blessing for us. The prophet Elisha was in the right location when he was sustained by the woman from Zeraphath amidst the famine. God has a way of multiplying the little resources that we have; like the song says, "Little is much when God is in it." The little meal in a barrel and the oil in the vessel stretched and multiplied as the prophet Elisha commanded her. It was by faith that the prophet's widow was able to pay off her debts by being obedient to the words of Elisha to pour the little oil that she had, and supernaturally the oil multiplied to pay off her debts. Beloved, it is here that we stand firm on faith in belief that God shall supply all our needs according to His riches in glory. Beloved, you may be experiencing a hard time financially; just remember to trust and have faith in God that He will make a way where there seems to be no way.

Much Prayer, Much Power

I can remember back in the year 2012 that after my encounter with God, I would pray in the morning, at lunch, and before bed. During these times of prayer I felt, as it were, that volts of electricity enveloped my entire being. Before my encounter with the Master, I never had a prayer life; I would pray at church prayer meetings, but I never had a personal relationship with God. During that period in time I felt the Holy Ghost pulling me to my knees to pray, and it was at that point that I had an experience and a personal relationship with the Almighty. There is an ecstasy with God that I experienced—the euphoria of the Holy Ghost. This experience was heaven on earth, a burning fire in my hands and in my feet. During these moments of prayer I had visions of God, high and lifted up, just like the prophets of old saw Him. However, one must pay an expensive price to see God, for no man can see God and live, because God's presence is too powerful for mere human beings to behold. The price is suffering, the price is isolation, the price is humility. Prayer not only changes things; prayer changes me. In my time spent with God, my very features started to change. As it were, the light of God started to shine from the inside out. If you want a deeper encounter with God, I encourage you to develop a prayer life that will propel you into His presence; lives will be changed, and the glory of God will be revealed. If you need chains to break and yokes to be destroyed, develop an attitude and posture of prayer, where one hour will seem like twenty minutes; where your spirit man and your inner being will grow. Jesus asked His disciples, "Could you not watch with me one hour?" (Matthew 26:40 ESV), And Jesus also encouraged His disciples to pray lest they enter into temptation. A strategy to avoid temptation is to pray to God to overcome temptation. The flesh will diminish, deplete, and start to die.

The prophets of old would build an altar to commune with God; we should always build an altar to get divine direction from God. Remember, beloved, that Jesus tore the veil that separated man from God, so now we have access to God through prayer. The concept of prayer also is relationship. Just as we have a relationship with our parents, God seeks to have a relationship with us, and the God who seems far-fetched and distant cannot become your best friend. God does not get tired of hearing our prayers; in fact, He delights when we come to Him in prayer. The scripture says that men must always pray and not faint. Prayer is our lifeline to God almighty, and it takes us into that secret place with God. Jesus gives the illustration of the woman and the unjust judge, that by the woman continuously coming to the judge, the judge gave her audience. We do not weary God by praying; He wants us to have a talk with Him, and God who sees you in secret will reward you openly. Remember the story of Paul and Silas: when they were imprisoned, they prayed and sang praises unto God, and God miraculously loosed their shackles and delivered them out of prison. You might be in bondage today, my friend; just begin to give God praise and pray your way out of the jail of anxiety, fear, lack, and distress. Remember the story of Peter: that prayer was being made by the church in a house, and the Lord sent His angel to deliver Peter out of prison, and the Bible says that the gates of the prison opened on their own accord. It is here that we see the power of corporate prayer. The damsel was astonished when she saw Peter, and it is here that, when God answers our prayers, we must be careful that we don't develop the attitude of unbelief, because God is a God who answers prayers. You may have been praying a long time and you haven't seen any results; keep on praying, beloved—God will answer, because God is an on-time God. Other people of different religious persuasions pray five times a day; as Christians we seem a bit timid to pray, and some may not even have a prayer life. We as believers must develop that Daniel spirit to open our spiritual windows and pray unto our one true and living God, the God of Abraham, Isaac, and Jacob, and Daniel's God will deliver us out of the mouths of the lions of persecution, turmoil, and distress.

Inferiority Complex

You might be struggling with feelings of inferiority—that you are not enough, that you're not smart enough, or you feel as if you don't have the wherewithal to accomplish the task that God has called you to do. Moses felt inferior when God gave him the call to lead the children of Israel out of Egypt. Moses wanted Aaron, his brother, to do the task, because Moses was slow of speech and he did not feel eloquent enough. God said to Moses, "Who has made man's mouth?" (Exodus 4:11 NKJV). God was just showing Moses that he wouldn't have to do the task alone, that God would be with him to be his mouth and give Moses the inspiration to speak to Pharaoh. See, God calls the base things, the weak things, the insufficient people; God doesn't call the qualified but He qualifies the called. You might not have a degree, or you might not have graduated from an Ivy League college, but God has a way of teaching us and giving us wisdom beyond our ability. Beloved, I have had those moments of insufficiency, where I didn't feel I was qualified to do what God has called me to do; but God wants us to partner with Him to get the task done. Just like the apostle Paul says, "Hear our calling, brethren: not many wise, not many noble are called, but God has chosen the foolish things, the base things, to confound the wisdom of the wise" (1 Corinthians 1:26 paraphrased). Gideon was called but felt inferior because he was the least of all his brethren and was poor, but the angel of the Lord called him "thou mighty man of valor" (Judges 6:12 KJV). God sees something in us that He can use, even though we may be poor. In the next verse Gideon said, "If God be with us, why has all this befallen us? Where are the miracles that our parents told us about?" Beloved, you may be wondering what is happening in your life—why the suffering? Why so much pain? But God calls us because He knows that there is a job to be done, there is an assignment that God wants us to accomplish. Jeremiah, when he was called, was but a child, but God calls young men because they are strong. You may feel like a child, and you don't think you have the education or the skills to do what God has called you to do; He will help you along the way and will walk you through the process. Noah got drunk; Moses murdered an Egyptian and had a speech impediment; Jacob stole his brother's birthright; David was a murderer and took Uriah's wife; however, God called David "a man after His own heart" (1 Samuel 13:14 NKJV). If God used all these imperfect people, why can't God use you?

Where Is Your Faith in God?

Faith is the hallmark of what we believe as Christians. For God is a Spirit that dwells outside of time; and without faith it is impossible to please God, for if we come to God, we must believe that He exists. No man has seen God any time, but we believe in a God who we cannot see. When we consider the heavens, the moon, and the stars, we know that there is a mastermind behind the cosmos, and it takes a belief that God is and that He exists. We can see the evidence of God's existence internally and externally. Internally, because we can feel Him moving on the altars of our hearts; externally, we believe because we see His creation, His handiwork. The Bible is another evidence that we have as proof that God is. He called imperfect men to reveal His nature, His ways, and His deeds to us. By faith Enoch was not, because the Lord took him, because Enoch walked with God by faith, not having seen God. But by faith Enoch believed God, and Enoch's experience was a type and shadow of the rapture. Abraham believed God, and it was counted to him as righteousness, because Abraham didn't have the law of Moses, but Abraham had faith in God, having not seen Him. Abraham was promised the land of Canaan as an inheritance and was promised a child, even though his wife Sarah was barren. God said that "in thee shall all nations be blessed" (Galatians 3:8 KJV). God told Abraham to look at the stars and so shall his heirs be, as the sand of the sea. Sarah was ninety and Abraham was a hundred, and it took faith to believe God; what was impossible can be made possible by faith. Scientifically, it was impossible for Sarah to conceive a child, being ninety years old. Sarah laughed at the promise that she would bear a child in her old age, and God's promise may seem comical, but when God makes a promise, you can stand on it. Abraham also had faith in God to believe, so that when God told him to offer up the promised seed, Isaac, as a sacrifice, Abraham went, not knowing the outcome. It is here that we must believe God's promise and take Him at His word. Just has the songwriter penned it, "You may not know how, you may not know when, but He'll do it again." Faith is the bridge that takes us to the throne room of God's presence. When we are on the bridge of life, the tendency for us is to fear. However, we should have hope in the fact that God made us a promise; He is able to fulfill that promise. It took faith for Noah to build an ark when he had not seen rain. I can imagine that the people were laughing at Noah as he built the ark, but Noah had faith in the words of God Almighty that it was going to rain.

By faith, God spared and saved Noah's household and the animals from the flood.

I've often wondered, how does one get saved, considering all the denominations that exist in Christendom? The Christian religion seems to be divided, and it could leave one in a quandary, wondering how to be saved. For the Pentecostals believe in the baptism of the Holy Spirit and being immersed in water in Jesus' name. The Trinitarians, including the Baptists, Methodists, Catholics, and Presbyterians, believe in baptism in the Father, the Son, and the Holy Spirit. Beloved, Christendom is in a quandary, and we as believers need to be united in faith and doctrine. Christianity is founded upon the Judeo-Christian ethic which says *Shema Israel Adonai elohenu Adonai Echad*, which is Hebrew for "Hear, O Israel: The Lord our God is one" (Deuteronomy 6:4 KJV). We as believers must understand that our God is One; He is not three, neither is God the second person in the Trinity; beloved, the God that we serve is One. God is the "I am" God, which is the ever-present, self-existing One. We must believe that God is, and that He is a rewarder of those that diligently seek Him. God cannot be placed under a microscope to find His DNA; however, faith is the means by which we get to God. Many scientists and philosophers have tried to find evidence of God, and they state that a loving God would not allow such evil like tornadoes and hurricanes and other natural disasters to occur, if God is loving. These philosophers state that a loving God would not allow such evil to happen to mankind. These scientists ask why He would want Abraham to sacrifice his only son. And they state that the Bible is hate literature. Beloved, we must understand that God is just and sovereign; He allows these natural disasters to occur. I want us to know that it is okay to question God; when Jesus was on the cross, He cried, "*Eli, Eli, lama sabachthani*," which means, "Father, Father, why hast thou forsaken me?" (Matthew 27:46 KJV). It is okay to ask God why.

Soteriology

I have often wondered about soteriology, which is the doctrine of salvation. We are saved by faith and not by works; it is not by works, lest any man should boast; it is the gift of God. Salvation is a gift, and all we have to do is to receive God's gift. The first step for salvation is repentance, which is an about turn from sin unto righteousness. Repentance is a military term—if you are headed toward destruction, you should change your mind and go in a different direction. It is with the mouth that man believes and with the mouth confession is made. In order to repent, one must first confess Jesus as Lord and Savior. The apostle Paul states that you must confess with your mouth and believe in your heart that God has raised Christ from the dead, and you shall be saved. We must understand that we must be born again; a rebirth is very vital for salvation. In John 3:1-3, Nicodemus asked Jesus, "What must I do to be saved?" Jesus replied, "You must be born again." One must be born of the water and of the Spirit in order to be saved. We were born in sin and sharpened in iniquity, and all of us have the Adamic nature and tendency to sin. "For all have sinned, and come short of the glory of God" (Romans 3:23 KJV). "If we say that we have no sin, we deceive ourselves, and the truth is not in us" (1 John 1:8 KJV). It is the blood of Jesus and the death of Christ on the cross that justifies us as believers. *Justified* means "just as if I had not sinned." For there is therefore now no condemnation to them that are in Christ Jesus. Christ did not die to condemn us, but He came to justify us. All our good deeds cannot measure up to God's standards of holiness, because man has a sin problem. After I've messed up, I often feel condemned and ashamed and guilty, but I'm reminded that God's grace is sufficient and we cannot out-sin God's grace. Jesus died for our sins, past, present, and future. Jesus cried "It is finished" when He was on the cross, which means that the debt that we owe as sinners was paid in full on Calvary. Jesus died for the entire world, for John 3:16 declares, "For God so loved the world that He gave His only begotten Son, that whoever believes in Him should not perish but have everlasting life" (NKJV). My friends, Jesus's love reached into to the vicissitudes of man's calamity and disdain, and the blood of Jesus covered the entire globe, including North America, South America, the Caribbean, Europe, Asia, and the Middle East. Christ's love and His salvific work on the cross covered everybody.

Fear Not

Fear and mental health issues seem to be on the rise, and people seem to be anxious about the circumstances they face. The scripture says that men's hearts shall fail them for fear in the latter days. The juxtaposition or contrast of fear is faith, and so we've got to have faith amidst the fearful and anxious situations in life. "Fear not" is written in scripture 365 times, which means God wants us not to fear every day of the year. It is here, when Christ gives us a command to go over on the other side like He told His disciples, that unexpected storms will arise. Just know that when Christ gives us a command, oftentimes He is testing us to see if we will believe or doubt that He is able to take us through the storms of life. Peter said, "Lord, if it is You, command me to come to you on the water" (Matthew 14:28 NKJV), and Peter began to walk on water, but Peter began to sink because of doubt and the boisterous winds and rain. On another occasion, Christ was in the inner part of the ship sleeping while there arose a storm. The question you might be asking is, why would Christ be asleep when something so fearful and threatening as a storm was on the horizon? Beloved, all we have to do is wake Jesus up and tell Him about our storm. He might seem to be asleep and not bothered or concerned about your storm; just get on your knees and tell the Master about the storm that you are faced with. God is looking for some "water walkers" to defy fear and walk on the waters of your fears and problems, knowing that the Lord is in the ship, and He is well able to take us over to the shore. One of my songs that I wrote is called "Fear Not," and the lyrics say, "Why are you so troubled, why are you soon overcome by this boisterous wave? He is in the ship, don't you worry, don't you fret, though the billows are high, though the storm is nigh." Beloved, "fear not" is a command by God because He knows that the trials of life will cause us to fear. Some people are afraid of heights; some are claustrophobic, having fear of close spaces; some are agoraphobic, which is fear of situations that cause panic and anxiety. Beloved, I have struggled in my life with panic attacks and anxiety, where I felt like my heart was racing and beating rapidly and it seemed terrifying. I had to learn to take those deep breaths, to inhale and exhale. Sometimes anxiety seems like it's the end of the world, but it's seeing danger, and with God and with time you will be back to equilibrium and balance before you know it.

I am reminded of the story of Lazarus: how Mary and Martha were perplexed about their brother Lazarus; how he died, and Jesus tarried three days, which according to Jewish custom is the time that the spirit would hover over the body. So Jesus made sure that the this Jewish custom was done away with so that a miracle could take place. "Jesus wept" (John 11:35 NKJV), which is the shortest verse in the Bible. Jesus weeps because of our dead situation, and He is full of compassion. Jesus stated, "I am glad for your sakes... that you may believe" (verse 15). I can see Jesus standing by the tomb of Lazarus as He cried, "Lazarus, come forth!" (verse 43) and then Lazarus, who was dead, got up, and the spirit returned to his body. My friend, I am writing this to extend your faith beyond the natural and to help you see in the supernatural all that God can do, because there is nothing too hard for God. So, you might have lost a loved one and you are dealing with grief—just know that there is hope for a child of Gideon who has transitioned from time to eternity; oh, yes indeed, there is hope for a soul that was born again and has experienced death. The apostle Paul admonished and encouraged the believers and the church that there are different bodies: there are heavenly bodies, which are the planets in the galaxy, celestial bodies. Paul encouraged the believers that one day death will be swallowed up in victory, and death shall have its final death; death indeed shall die, according to the book of Revelation. The apostle Paul declared, "Behold, I tell you a mystery: we shall not all sleep" (1 Corinthians 15:51 NKJV), which is *yeshen* in the Hebrew, "this mortal must put on immortality" (verse 53). So, I would like to encourage you to know that there is life after death, and that death is just a portal to take us into the presence of almighty God. The tendency for us when we have lost a loved one is to be angry at God, but we've got to learn to say "it is well," like the Shunammite did in the time of the prophet Elisha. Jesus told the people that Jarius's daughter was not dead, but asleep; when Christ said that they laughed at Him, but Jesus put all of them out. See, beloved, we have got to shut the door on unbelief if we are going to see the miraculous; we can have God silence the noise of unbelief.

Take Not Thy Holy Spirit

After I had experienced, as it were, an Ichabod, I often felt this void and emptiness on the inside. It occurred to me that the anointing is God's anointing, and He can take the anointing away and withdraw Himself so we can pant after God. Israel was in a dire strait when Israel had lost the ark of the covenant. And so, *Ichabod* simply means "the glory has departed." Oh, beloved, we need to not lose the presence of God, because if we do, it gives the enemy an opportunity to attack. It might seem as if you are losing the war in your life or in your marriage; all you have to do is to invite God's presence into your circumstances, and the Lord's presence will intervene. As a result of King Saul's disobedience, the presence of God had left him because of his pride and arrogance. King Saul consulted the witch of Endor to see if he could get a word from God, but his efforts in getting a word from God left him even more isolated and separated from God's presence. Beloved, we need God's glory with us; we need to hear the voice of God clearly so we know what decision we ought to make. Samson had another experience where the glory of God had left him; Samson lost his strength because he had aligned himself with Delilah, who was a Philistine. It is here that we have to be careful about who we align and attach ourselves to, and we should not forget the covenant that God has made with us. We need to remember that after the anointing of God departs, if we truly repent, the anointing can return. Samson, even though he lost his strength, his strength was regained; and Samson destroyed more Philistines in his death than in his life. Beloved, you might feel empty and feel as though God has gone on a far journey; your anointing and God's glory can return if you truly seek the Lord with a true and sincere heart. King David, after he had sinned against God, confessed his sins against God in Psalm 51, and the most vital thing that David petitioned God was for God not to take His Holy Spirit from him. After we have fallen from grace into sin, we need to ask God to create in us a clean heart and renew a right spirit within us. We must understand also that there are consequences to our actions, because David, even though he repented, lost his male child, and Absalom wanted to overthrow David from being king over Israel. We have to be mindful of our actions that allow the consequences of sin to follow us.

I've had my share of battles with depression, where life seems hopeless and meaningless. I just want you to know that you are not alone. Some might have even contemplated ending their life. I just want you to know that I have been there, where things seem dark and you say, like Job, "Oh, that I knew where I might find Him" (Job 23:3 NKJV). Some of the greatest men in the Bible have battled with depression. Jeremiah said, "Oh that my head were waters, and mine eyes a fountain of tears" (Jeremiah 9:1 KJV), that he may weep over the situation that Israel was in. Jeremiah, who was also known as the weeping prophet, said that he did not want to preach or prophesy anymore. But Jeremiah said it felt like fire shut up within his bones. Throughout Jeremiah's ministry, he could have given up the prophetic call and mandate that was on his life, but he persevered even though he was imprisoned. Depression seems to be taboo and less talked about even in the church, where some Christians believe that if you have depression then it means that you are possessed with a devil. It is also important to get help from a therapist, especially a Christian therapist, because we all need godly counsel and help to get out of the dark places we find ourselves in. We need to put an end to another life that seems hopeless, and that soul who is not wanting to live anymore as a result of the cares of life. So, I encourage you, beloved, to find hope in Christ and in the scriptures, for in them we find hope and solace for the journey ahead. The verse that has encouraged me is, "Thou wilt keep him in perfect peace, whose mind is stayed on Thee" (Isaiah 26:3 KJV). We have to keep our minds on God and His words, because the enemy is like a roaring lion, seeking whom he may devour, and in order to counteract the tactics of the evil one we have to keep our minds stayed on Christ. God is a keeper, and if God has kept me thus far, He is able to keep you too. Another scripture that has kept me is Jeremiah 29:11 (KJV) which states, "For I know the plans I have for you, thoughts of peace and not of evil, to give you an expected end." God's thoughts toward us are good, and before we were conceived in our mother's womb God knew us and ordained us and created us with a purpose. So, I encourage you to live on and keep going, and in the words of my father, "Don't die until you're dead." You are not a mistake, and God has a plan for your life; though things may seem dark and dismal, "Trust in the Lord with all your heart, and lean not on your own understanding; in all your ways acknowledge Him, and He shall direct your paths" (Proverbs 3:5-6 NKJV).

The Ministry
Is Not a Game

There seems to be a lot of evil in the world. The apostle Paul says, "When I would do good, evil is present" (Romans 7:21 paraphrased). Life is comprised of the juxtaposition of light and darkness, good and evil, up and down, left and right, God and devil, heaven and hell. So, if there is evil, there must be good that follows. It is with this that I say that the ministry is not a game. Maybe you feel the call of God upon your heart, and you feel called to the ministry. The ministry is not for the faint of heart or the weak or the timid, but God is looking for soldiers. For we wrestle not against flesh and blood, but we are at war with principalities and powers. It is very imperative that you cover your children under the blood of Jesus, just as the children of Israel were told to put the blood upon the lintels and upon the doorposts of the house, so we should pray and apply the blood of Jesus upon our families. We have an opposing force who doesn't play fair; neither does he play games, and there is a battle for our souls. Our soul is very valuable to us and to God, because our soul gives us God-consciousness and gives us world awareness. The soul is the seat of our emotions, and that is what enemy is after. God breathed the *Ruach,* the breath, into man, and man became a living soul. The wicked one was right there in the book of Genesis, trying to sever the relationship that man has with God. In the cool of the day God communed with man, but the evil one wanted to sever the ties and bonds that mankind has with the Lord God of Israel. We were created in the image God, so the evil one wants to distort our physical features, because every time the enemy looks at us he sees God's image. The enemy has over six thousand years of experience, and he was created as the morning star—he was beautiful, until iniquity was found in him. In him were pipes and precious stones; he was the praise and worship leader in heaven until the enemy looked at his beauty and said that he shall ascend above the throne of God—the wicked one wanted to be like God. And one third of the angels that worked with the enemy were kicked out of heaven. So, the devil and his demons now work in the atmospheric heaven, and there is a prince demon that hovers over every region. I must say, I was ignorant to the devil's devices when I was twenty-four years old and I started to preach. I was ignorant to the fact that the wicked one is after preachers, and especially pastors' children; so, if you know any "PKs," or pastor's kids, continue to pray for us, because the devil doesn't like us and the wicked one tries to attack the ministry by attacks on the pastor's children. I encourage anyone that feels called to ministry to have a prayer life—and most importantly, to have a balance, to learn to balance the natural and the spiritual, to have a balanced diet and work out or go to the gym. And refrain from fasting the day that you are going to preach, as your blood sugar can fall. I had to learn from experience when I went on a twenty-one day fast and I went into the spirit realm, where I was attacked physically and spiritually, where my blood sugar fell and I had to be hospitalized. As they say, the Jews have zeal but not according to knowledge, so we as believers must have zeal but also have knowledge to know that we are not spiritual beings but we are, most importantly, physical.

The Fields Are Ripe

I have a deep passion for evangelism and outreach, where we and the saints from my church would go door to door and hand out tracts inviting people to church. The reception wasn't as receptive as I had hoped, but we visited the neighborhoods around the perimeter of my church. Jesus said to His disciples, "Go into all the world and preach the gospel to every creature" (Mark 16:15 NKJV). This was a command by Christ for us as believers to reach out to the hurting, to the lost, to the poor and destitute. There should be a hunger, a passion, and a desire to win the lost souls in our communities and reach them with the Word of God. The apostles gave their lives for the ministry, and they stood up against the naysayers and those that rejected their teaching. We should develop that persuasion and fervor to say that if it costs us our lives, we are not going to relent until all the world hears the gospel of Jesus Christ. Some individuals are addicted to drugs, some folks are homeless, and some are hopeless, and we have been commissioned by Christ to help the hurting and reach the dying and to tell them that them that Jesus Christ is the only solution to their problems. Jesus calls the Church the light of the world, and we should not hide the light; but we as believers should shine that light in this dark world. Christ calls us the salt of the earth, and as salt we preserve this world from the ruins of darkness and evil. Jesus told Peter to cast his net to catch fish, and at the word of Jesus, Peter was able to catch a multitude of fish. Fish here represent men, and the harvest that is out in the world; the net represents the Word of God and the means by which we use tactical strategies to reach the lost.

The fields are ripe and ready for harvest, and the Lord Jesus is looking for laborers in the vineyard to win souls for the kingdom. Jesus is Lord of the harvest, and it is indeed reaping time, considering all that is happening in the world. And just as the animals picked up the vibration in the time of the flood, so people are picking up the vibration of the perilous times that we are living in. The prodigal son spent all his inheritance on riotous living, but came to his senses and returned to his father's house. But what is paramount is that the father was waiting for his son to return, and saw his son afar off and hugged him and had a feast for his son. So in the natural, so in the spiritual, where God is waiting for His children to return to the ark of safety, where in the Father's kingdom are many mansions and there be a feast prepared for the harvest of souls that return. God is after the one lost sheep, where the shepherd leaves the ninety and nine and goes after the one lost sheep that had strayed away. So, Christ being the Shepherd goes after us, and though we stray away from the church, Jesus is waiting patiently and is pursuing the lost that have strayed. Beloved, you might have strayed away from the house of God, but Christ is waiting for His sons and daughters to return home. So, just keep praying for your children who have strayed and have become backsliders; just know that the seed of the Word of the Lord has been planted in their hearts, and though they stray, they will return to their rightful place in God.

The Heart of Man

The Bible states in Jeremiah 17:9 that the heart of man is desperately wicked; who can know it? The gifted and anointed have to go through trials and hatred by the people that are closest to them. The gifted will always have people who are jealous of them because of the call of God that is on their lives. The devil will even use family members, people who you confide in, to try to abort the destiny that God has for you. It is here that Cain killed Abel because Cain's sacrifice was rejected, and Abel's sacrifice was accepted. Joseph's brothers hated him because of the dream that God gave him, that the son, the moon, and the eleven stars would bow down to Joseph. Joseph's dream was indicative of him saving is brothers and parents because of the drought in Egypt. Joseph's brothers lied about him and threw him in the pit and sold him to the Midianites in Egypt. However, God's hand was upon Joseph, and God's promise, providence, and destiny were upon Joseph's life. Joseph went from the palace into prison, and from prison to the head of Potiphar's house. Joseph confronted his brothers finally and said, "What you meant for evil, God turned around for my good" (Genesis 50:20 paraphrased). Through all that Joseph went through, he maintained his integrity.

People may have lied about you, mistreated you; just know that the battle belongs to the Lord. You don't have to get even with those who did you wrong; just know it's God's battle to fight. Pharaoh wanted to kill the firstborn in Egypt; Saul wanted to kill David; Herod wanted to kill the male children because he was threatened by Jesus. Judas betrayed Jesus; Peter denied Jesus. The Pharisees wanted to destroy Christ. The Jews cried, "Release Barabbas!" and had Jesus crucified. Sanballat and Tobiah wanted to stop the building of the temple. Two men withstood Moses. Jezebel wanted to kill Elijah. Hitler wanted to kill the Jews. Daniel was hated and was thrown in the den of lions. The three Hebrew boys were thrown in the fire. See, beloved, gifted people are always under attack; the key is to maintain our composure and our integrity when we are hated by the ones that are closest to us. It's a sort of betrayal when the people that you love the most are envious and jealous of you. The key is to maintain your integrity in God; it is said that "church hurt" is the worst hurt, and some of us have been hurt by a lie or a rumor. Just let God be the vindicator. Just remember that the Christian life is a life of the cross, and if Christ, who was sinless and blameless, went through the most embarrassing sort of betrayal, who are we not to go through our cross and persecution?

Let us pray for the peace of Jerusalem and for the nation of Israel, as Israel is God's chosen people. We are currently living in the dispensation of grace, where God is now dealing with Gentiles, who are non-Jews. After the times of the Gentiles, God will turn back to the nation of Israel. Blindness has happened to Israel, as some Jews are still waiting for the Messiah to come to save them. God has not appointed the Church unto wrath, as God will rapture the Church and those who have not received Christ will be appointed unto wrath in the tribulation. The tribulation will be difficult to endure, as God will begin to pour out judgment on those who have rejected Christ. Beloved, now is the opportune time to be saved and give our lives in surrender to Christ. The one hundred and forty-four thousand Jews from each of the twelve tribes of Israel will be saved during the tribulation. If we will not receive Christ in the grace dispensation, it will be very difficult to surrender in the times of the tribulation, because the lawless one will persecute those who believe in Jesus Christ. The scripture says that Israel will be hated of all men for God's sake, as Israel had been through much persecution and enslavement by Egypt in the book of Exodus for four hundred years. Many Jews were annihilated during World War II in the holocaust. The scripture says, "I will bless those who bless you, and I will curse him who curses you" (Genesis 12:3 NKJV). So, there is a blessing that comes from almighty God when we pray and support the nation of Israel. I am very proud of my Jewish Jamaican ancestry on my father's side of the family and will continue to support Israel and be a beacon for the Jewish diaspora in Jamaica and worldwide.

Times and Seasons

———————

Time is very precious and valuable; time cannot be regained when lost. The Bible says in Ephesians 5:16 to redeem the time, because the days are evil. *Redeem* means "to make use of." The Psalmist David asks God in Psalm 90:12 to teach us to number our days, so we may apply our hearts to knowledge. Solomon says in Ecclesiastes 3:1-8 that there is a time for everything under the sun. There is a time to be born, a time to die, a time to reap, a time to sow; for everything there is a time and a season. Time teaches us to forgive a person who did us wrong, to let the past go and move towards the future. *Chronos* speaks of calendar time; *Kyros* speaks of when God steps out of eternity and steps into time to make known His deeds to humanity. The *Kyros* is very essential because we want God to perform a miracle in our lives, and in the fullness of time, God will manifest and make His deeds known in this and the current generation. Gen Z and Millennials are full of questions: why can't we see God? and who created God? and why do we have to go to church? and why do we have to dress a certain way? Beloved, it is time for God to reveal Himself in this generation, and if we don't see the manifested glory of God in this generation, we will have a generation that doesn't know God and a generation that doesn't want anything to do with God.

We live in a world that is dominated by materialism, and the culture seems to be a self-centered and self-aggrandized society. It seems to be that the world is putting a priority on the material instead of the spiritual. The scripture says, "What will it profit a man if he gains the whole world, and loses his own soul?" (Mark 8:36 NKJV). Our souls are very valuable, and our souls belong to God. However, people seem to be selling out for gains in money and fame. The entertainment industry seems to be filled with folks who are merchandising their souls in return for wealth and riches. Our soul is valued far more than any riches that the industry and the world can amass. We should let the world and the industry know: "soul not for sale." For God shall bring into judgment every secret thing, whether they be good or whether they be evil. I can recall the story in Luke 12 of the rich man who amassed all his goods and laid them up for many years, and he said, "I will say to my soul, eat drink and be merry" (verse 19), but that night his soul was required of him. The focal point should not be how much riches we can gain in this life, but we should have compassion on the poor and the homeless, and the widows, and those who are in need. Beloved, we are mere custodians of what God has blessed us with; they are just borrowed. We should have an eternal perspective on this life; life should be about righteousness, peace, and joy in the Holy Ghost. Many people have wealth and money but no peace, and some are miserable and depressed because life does not consist in the abundance of things that we possess. If you want true peace, it can only be found in Jesus Christ. Christ will give you "peace that passeth all [human] understanding" (Philippians 4:7 KJV). Solomon was very wealthy, and when he calculated it, he said in Ecclesiastes 12:13 that all is vanity, and the conclusion of the whole matter is to fear God and keep His commandments.

Beloved, you have been through a lot and you have faced many trials, but praise will take you through the storm; whatever you're going through, just remember praise will take you through every circumstance. You might have lost a loved one and you are grieving; don't forget to get down on your knees and petition the throne room of grace, and pray and praise your way in the midst of what you are going through. God is the conductor of this grand symphony of life, and God has the baton, and He is the conductor of every facet of your life. Some of my favorite gospel songs have brought me through some hard times; gospel music has kept me through some dark and dismal times of my life. The enemy has tried to stop my praise, and I am determined to give God the glory in spite of what I am going through. The enemy will try to steal your dance, and he will try to muzzle your praise, but you have to have a determination like David said, "I will bless the Lord at all times" (Psalm 34:1 KJV). His praise should always be upon our lips. Many great composers such as Johann Sebastian Bach and Mozart have penned many great musical pieces, but at the end of their musical careers they composed many masterful pieces in dedication to our great God and King. One piece that Mozart composed is called "Kyrie Eleison," which is Latin for "Lord, have mercy." Oh, friends, we need the mercies of God, so our prayer should be, "Lord, have mercy in the *Dies Irie*," or day of wrath. Another classical piece by Mozart is called "Lacrimosa," which in the Latin means "to cry." Friends, there are many things that would cause us to cry; however, don't forget that tears are a language that God understands. So, keep on trusting and keep on believing, knowing that He who has begun a good work in you will perform it till the day of Jesus Christ.

Milton Keynes UK
Ingram Content Group UK Ltd.
UKHW020919211124
3009UKWH00037B/126